# THE CAPTAIN COOK COOKBOOK

## BY
## ROBERT STEFFY

## ILLUSTRATED BY
## FRANK ANSLEY

PUBLISHED BY
DETERMINED PRODUCTIONS, INC.
BOX 2150
SAN FRANCISCO
CALIFORNIA 94126

Library of Congress Catalog Card No. 78-64499
ISBN No. 0-915696-11-8
Printed in the United States of America

# TABLE OF CONTENTS

## Asparagus in Prosciutto

TAKE 4 LARGE ASPARAGUS SPEARS PER PERSON. PEEL LOWER STEMS AND CUT INTO 5 INCH LENGTHS —

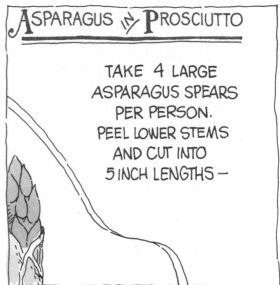

SIMMER IN BOILING WATER FOR 5 MINUTES. DRAIN.

WRAP EACH PIECE WITH PROSCIUTTO. PLACE IN A BUTTERED AU GRATIN DISH AND DRIZZLE WITH MELTED BUTTER.

SPRINKLE WITH PARMESAN CHEESE AND BAKE IN A 400° OVEN FOR 5 MINUTES.

I CAN'T WAIT.

WE'LL MAKE **AVOCADO WITH SWEET-SOUR SAUCE** BY FIRST SELECTING **3** NICE AVOCADOS.

...THEN WE'LL HEAT **6** TABLESPOONS BUTTER, **6** TABLESPOONS VINEGAR, **6** TABLESPOONS SUGAR, AND **6** TABLESPOONS WORCESTERSHIRE SAUCE.

AT THE SAME TIME, COOK **6** SLICES OF BACON UNTIL CRISP.

. AND POUR INTO UNPEELED AVOCADO HALVES (ONE HALF FOR EACH PERSON).

FINALLY, TOP WITH CRUMBLED BACON.

SERVES SIX!

## TO MAKE DELICIOUS
# WHITE BEANS WITH TUNA
### CATCH:

- 2 CUPS COOKED NAVY BEANS
- ½ BERMUDA ONION, THINLY SLICED
- 1 7-OZ. CAN TUNA IN OIL
- ⅓ CUP OLIVE OIL
- 2 TEASPOONS RED WINE VINEGAR
  SALT TO TASTE
  CHOPPED PARSLEY
  PEPPER

SOAK ONION SLICES IN TWO CHANGES OF WATER FOR 1 HOUR, DRAIN. MIX BEANS, ONION AND TUNA WITH OLIVE OIL, VINEGAR AND SALT.

PLACE ON SERVING PLATES. GARNISH WITH COARSELY GROUND BLACK PEPPER AND CHOPPED PARSLEY.

CHEESE!

### Cheddar Cheese wafers

½ POUND CHEDDAR CHEESE, GRATED
¼ POUND BUTTER
½ TEASPOON SALT
1¼ CUPS FLOUR
½ TEASPOON DRY MUSTARD
CAYENNE PEPPER TO TASTE

COMBINE INGREDIENTS AND KNEAD INTO LOG SHAPE. WRAP AND CHILL. CUT INTO ¼ INCH SLICES AND...

... BAKE IN A 350° OVEN FOR 10 MINUTES OR UNTIL BROWNED.

FOR A FORMIDABLE **CHICKEN LIVER PÂTÉ** :

4 TBSP. BUTTER
½ lb. MUSHROOMS, CHOPPED
1 lb. CHICKEN LIVERS
1 TSP. GARLIC SALT
1 TSP. PAPRIKA

⅓ CUP GREEN ONIONS, FINELY CHOPPED
⅓ CUP DRY WHITE WINE
3 DROPS HOT PEPPER SAUCE
PINCH OF DILL WEED
¼ lb. BUTTER

J'aime le pâté !

SAUTÉ MUSHROOMS AND CHICKEN LIVERS FOR 5 MINUTES WITH BUTTER, GARLIC SALT, PAPRIKA AND ONIONS. ADD WINE, DILL WEED AND HOT PEPPER SAUCE. COVER AND LET SIMMER 8 MINUTES.

WHEN COOL, PUT THROUGH A FOOD MILL. BLEND IN THE BUTTER AND TASTE FOR SALT. PACK IN JARS AND CHILL OVERNIGHT.

# SPICY CHICKEN WINGS

1 POUND CHICKEN WINGS
2 TABLESPOONS SOY SAUCE
1 TABLESPOON SHERRY WINE
1 TABLESPOON FRESH MINCED GINGER
1 TABLESPOON CORIANDER

THE HARD PART IS THE WINGS.

COMBINE INGREDIENTS AND MARINATE OVERNIGHT. PLACE IN A PAN FITTED WITH A RACK AND BAKE IN A 350° OVEN FOR 45 MINUTES, BASTING TWICE.

WE'VE EARNED OUR WINGS

# EGGS
### WITH
# CURRY SAUCE

4 TABLESPOONS BUTTER
1/2 CUP MINCED ONION
3 TABLESPOONS CURRY POWDER
4 TABLESPOONS FLOUR
2 CUPS SCALDED MILK
  SALT, PEPPER, LEMON JUICE
4 EGGS, HARD COOKED
  AND PEELED
  PARMESAN CHEESE

MELT BUTTER IN SAUCE PAN. ADD ONION AND COOK UNTIL TRANSPARENT. ADD CURRY POWDER AND FLOUR. COOK 2 MINUTES.

ADD SCALDED MILK, ALL AT ONCE, AND BEAT WITH A WHISK UNTIL SMOOTH AND THICK, 5 MINUTES. SEASON TO TASTE WITH SALT, PEPPER AND LEMON JUICE.

CUT EGGS IN HALF, REMOVE AND MASH YOLKS WITH ENOUGH OF THE SAUCE TO MAKE THEM SMOOTH.

STUFF HALVES WITH THE YOLK MIXTURE AND PLACE 2 FOR EACH PERSON IN INDIVIDUAL RAMEKINS.

MASK EGGS WITH THE REMAINING SAUCE AND SPRINKLE WITH PARMESAN CHEESE. BAKE IN A 350° OVEN UNTIL BUBBLY (15 MINUTES).

MAKES FOR A GREAT FIRST COURSE.

OR A BETTER BRUNCH.

F. ANSLEY

# DIP or DUNK

½ CUP MAYONNAISE
½ CUP SOUR CREAM
1 TEASPOON PARSLEY, MINCED
1 TEASPOON DILL WEED
1 TEASPOON GREEN ONION, MINCED
1 TEASPOON BEAU MONDE SEASONING

MIX ALL TOGETHER AND SERVE WITH CHIPS OR RAW VEGETABLE SPEARS.

¡GUACAMOLE!

TAKE 3 RIPE AVOCADOS, PEEL AND MASH THEM.

MIX IN 3 CHOPPED, CANNED CHILIES, 3 CHOPPED GREEN ONIONS..

CHILIES

ADD JUICE OF ONE LEMON, SALT AND HOT PEPPER SAUCE TO TASTE.

¡AY CARAMBA! IT'S GREAT WITH TORTILLAS OR CHIPS.

## NAVY BEAN SOUP

### U.S. NAVY SOUP ROSTER

- 3 ONIONS, MEDIUM, CHOPPED
- 2 CARROTS, PEELED AND DICED
- 2 CUPS CELERY, CHOPPED
- 2 TABLESPOONS OIL
- 2 CUPS NAVY BEANS, SOAKED OVERNIGHT
- 2 HOCKS, HAM
- 1 TOMATO, CHOPPED
- ½ TEASPOON THYME
- ½ TEASPOON OREGANO
- 2½ QUARTS WATER
  SALT AND PEPPER TO TASTE

BRING TO A BOIL, COVER AND SIMMER FOR 2 HOURS. REMOVE HAM HOCKS AND SHRED MEAT. RETURN TO SOUP POT AND TASTE FOR SEASONING.

SAUTÉ ONIONS, CARROTS, AND CELERY IN OIL UNTIL ONIONS ARE TRANSPARENT. TRANSFER TO SOUP KETTLE AND ADD OTHER INGREDIENTS.

ALL HANDS TO THE GALLEY! I THINK IT'S READY!

## →CAPTAIN COOK'S BORSCH←

6 CUPS WATER
1 POUND BEEF BRISKET, CUT INTO 6 PIECES
2 MEDIUM ONIONS, SLICED
2 CELERY STALKS, CUT INTO 1-INCH PIECES
4 MEDIUM BEETS, PEELED AND SLICED
2 MEDIUM BEETS, PEELED AND GRATED
4 CARROTS, PEELED AND SLICED
1 SMALL HEAD OF CABBAGE CUT INTO WEDGES
1 BAY LEAF
1 TABLESPOON SALT
1 6 OZ. CAN TOMATO PASTE
2 TABLESPOONS VINEGAR
1 TABLESPOON SUGAR
2 TEASPOONS SALT
1 CUP SOUR CREAM

**1** IN A LARGE KETTLE, PUT THE WATER, BEEF, ONIONS, CELERY, SLICED BEETS, CARROTS, CABBAGE, BAY LEAF AND SALT. BRING TO BOIL, COVER AND SIMMER FOR 2 HOURS. SKIM OFF FAT. ADD THE GRATED BEETS, TOMATO PASTE, VINEGAR, SUGAR, SALT AND SIMMER FOR 10 MINUTES. TOP WITH A SPOON OF SOUR CREAM.

# CAPTAIN COOK'S SOUP

1 16-oz. can tomatoes
2/3 can water
1 large onion, sliced
3 stalks celery, sliced
2 carrots, peeled and sliced
1/2 green pepper, chopped
2 tbsp. pickling spice
2 10½-oz. cans consommé
3/4 can dry sherry
Parmesan cheese, grated

①. SIMMER TOMATOES, WATER, ONION, CELERY, CARROTS, PEPPER, AND PICKLING SPICE FOR 30 MINUTES.

②. PUT THROUGH FOOD MILL.

③. ADD CONSOMMÉ AND SHERRY!

HEAT AND SERVE WITH PARMESAN CHEESE.

19

# CRANBERRY BEAN SOUP

| | |
|---|---|
| 2 | CUPS CRANBERRY BEANS |
| 1½ | QUARTS WATER |
| 1 | TEASPOON SALT |
| ¼ | TEASPOON PEPPER |
| 1 | TABLESPOON BUTTER |
| 2 | TABLESPOONS OIL |
| 2 | ONIONS, CHOPPED |
| 1 | CLOVE GARLIC, MINCED |
| 1 | CARROT, SHREDDED |
| 1 | TEASPOON BASIL |
| ½ | TEASPOON THYME |
| 1 | TEASPOON SUMMER SAVORY |
| ¼ | TEASPOON DRY MUSTARD |
| 1 | TABLESPOON WORCESTERSHIRE SAUCE |
| 2 | TABLESPOONS DRY SHERRY WINE |

SOAK BEANS OVERNIGHT IN WATER. DRAIN AND ADD 1½ QUARTS WATER, SALT AND PEPPER. PUT ON MEDIUM HEAT.

MELT BUTTER WITH OIL AND SAUTÉ ONIONS AND GARLIC FOR 10 MINUTES. ADD NEXT FOUR INGREDIENTS AND SAUTÉ FOR 5 MINUTES MORE.

ADD TO BEANS, COVER AND SIMMER FOR 3 HOURS. REMOVE HALF OF BEANS AND MASH THEM. RETURN TO SOUP POT WITH MUSTARD AND WORCESTERSHIRE SAUCE.

MASHER!

TASTE FOR SEASONING. BRING TO HEAT. BEFORE SERVING ADD THE SHERRY WINE BUT DO NOT BOIL.

THIS IS VERY GOOD AND INEXPENSIVE. A BUDGET STRETCHER. SERVE WITH FRENCH BREAD AND A SALAD AND A GLASS OF WINE..

.. OR TWO?

HELLO! ..SAY.. WE'RE MAKING

# LENTIL SOUP

AND WE'RE GOING TO NEED:

2 CUPS DRIED LENTILS
2½ QUARTS WATER
¼ CUP DICED SALT PORK
¾ CUP CHOPPED CARROTS
¾ CUP CHOPPED ONIONS
¾ CUP CHOPPED CELERY
1 CLOVE GARLIC, MINCED
1 HAM HOCK
1 BAY LEAF
2 WHOLE CLOVES
   SALT AND PEPPER
4 FRANKFURTERS, SLICED
   CHOPPED PARSLEY

YOU GOT IT!

PUT LENTILS AND WATER IN A LARGE KETTLE. SAUTÉ THE SALT PORK FOR 5 MINUTES. ADD THE VEGETABLES AND COOK 10 MINUTES.

ADD TO THE LENTILS WITH THE HAM HOCK, BAY LEAF AND CLOVES. BRING TO A BOIL AND SIMMER GENTLY FOR 2 HOURS. REMOVE THE HAM HOCK AND SHRED THE MEAT.

FORCE HALF THE LENTILS THROUGH A FOOD MILL. RETURN TO THE POT WITH THE HAM MEAT AND FRANK-FURTERS.

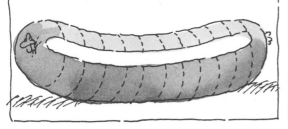

TASTE FOR SALT AND PEPPER. BRING TO A BOIL. SERVE WITH CHOPPED PARSLEY.

## CAPTAIN COOK'S MINESTRONE

½ POUND LEAN SALT PORK
¼ CUP OLIVE OIL
2 ONIONS, SLICED
3 CLOVES GARLIC
½ POUND WHITE BEANS, SOAKED OVERNIGHT
3 QUARTS WATER
½ TEASPOON BASIL
⅓ TEASPOON THYME
⅓ TEASPOON ROSEMARY
2 CARROTS, PEELED AND SLICED
2 TURNIPS, PEELED AND SLICED
4 ZUCCHINI, SLICED
3 TOMATOES, PEELED, SEEDED AND CHOPPED
1 SMALL HEAD CABBAGE, SHREDDED
1 SMALL BUNCH CELERY, SLICED
½ CUP MACARONI
PARMESAN CHEESE, GRATED

CUT SALT PORK INTO ½ INCH CUBES AND SAUTÉ UNTIL GOLDEN. DISCARD FAT. ADD ¼ CUP OLIVE OIL AND SAUTÉ ONIONS AND GARLIC UNTIL TRANSPARENT.

ADD DRAINED BEANS AND 3 QUARTS WATER. SEASON WITH BASIL, THYME AND ROSEMARY. COVER AND SIMMER 2 HOURS.

DISCARD GARLIC. ADD CARROTS AND TURNIPS AND COOK FOR ANOTHER 20 MINUTES. ADD ZUCCHINI, TOMATOES, CABBAGE, CELERY AND MACARONI AND BOIL VIGOROUSLY FOR 15 MINUTES.

TASTE FOR SEASONINGS. SERVE WITH PARMESAN CHEESE.

3 CUPS MILK
1 CUP CREAM
1 QUART OYSTERS
  SALT AND PEPPER
6 TABLESPOONS BUTTER
  CHOPPED PARSLEY

OYSTER STEW!

TIME TO GET THE OYSTERS OUT OF BED!

BRING MILK, CREAM AND OYSTER LIQUOR TO A BOIL. ADD OYSTERS AND RETURN TO BOIL.

SEASON WITH SALT AND PEPPER. LADLE INTO HEATED SOUP BOWLS AND ADD A PAT OF BUTTER TO EACH. SPRINKLE WITH CHOPPED PARSLEY AND SERVE.

F. ANSLEY

THIS FOG IS THICKER THAN..

..SPLIT PEA SOUP!

1½ CUPS DRIED GREEN SPLIT PEAS SOAKED OVERNIGHT
1 HAM HOCK
1 LARGE ONION, CHOPPED
3 STALKS CELERY, CHOPPED
2 QUARTS COLD WATER
1 BAY LEAF
  SALT AND PEPPER
1 LARGE GARLIC OR POLISH SAUSAGE

DRAIN THE PEAS AND PLACE IN A LARGE SOUP POT WITH THE HAM HOCK, ONION, CELERY, BAY LEAF AND WATER. BRING TO A BOIL AND SKIM OFF FOAM THAT FORMS ON TOP.

SIMMER GENTLY FOR 2 HOURS. REMOVE HAM HOCK AND SKIM THE FAT FROM THE SOUP. CUT THE MEAT FROM THE HAM HOCK AND RETURN IT TO THE SOUP!

TASTE FOR SEASONING. SLICE SAUSAGE AND ADD IT TO SOUP. SIMMER FOR ANOTHER 5 MINUTES AND SERVE.

FIRST WE'LL NEED TO GATHER UP SOME NICE VEGETABLES.

## CAPTAIN COOK'S VEGETABLE SOUP

½ CUP CHOPPED ONION
2 CLOVES GARLIC, MINCED
3 TABLESPOONS OIL
1½ POUNDS BEEF STEW MEAT, CUT IN SMALL PIECES
SALT AND PEPPER TO TASTE
FLOUR FOR DREDGING
1 10½ OZ. CAN CONSOMMÉ
1 10½ OZ. CAN CHICKEN BROTH
2 QUARTS WATER
½ CUP CHOPPED PARSLEY

1 CUP GREEN BEANS, SLICED
1 CUP CARROTS, PEELED & SLICED
1 CUP CELERY, SLICED
1 8 OZ. CAN TOMATO SAUCE
1 CUP PEAS
3 ZUCCHINI, SLICED
½ HEAD CABBAGE SHREDDED
1 8¾ OZ. CAN KIDNEY BEANS, DRAINED

IN A SAUTÉ PAN, COOK THE ONIONS AND GARLIC IN OIL UNTIL TRANSPARENT. PUT IN SOUP KETTLE.

IN SAME SAUTÉ PAN, BROWN THE BEEF THAT HAS BEEN DREDGED IN SEASONED FLOUR.

ADD TO KETTLE WITH CONSOMMÉ, CHICKEN BROTH, WATER, PARSLEY, GREEN BEANS, CARROTS, CELERY AND TOMATO SAUCE.

BRING TO BOIL AND SIMMER FOR 1½ HOURS.

WHICH WAY TO THE SOUP KITCHEN?

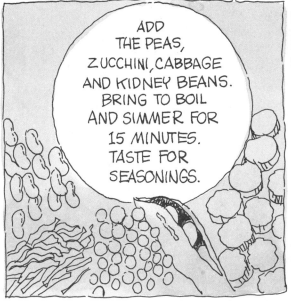

ADD THE PEAS, ZUCCHINI, CABBAGE AND KIDNEY BEANS. BRING TO BOIL AND SIMMER FOR 15 MINUTES. TASTE FOR SEASONINGS.

FINALLY, ENJOY!

# CLAMS AND RICE

**F**IRST GET ABOUT 3 POUNDS OF CLAMS IN SHELLS.
THEN SCRUB AND SOAK CLAMS IN COLD WATER FOR 1 HOUR.

**T**HEN DIG UP..

1 CUP GREEN ONIONS, SLICED

1 LARGE CLOVE GARLIC, CRUSHED

½ CUP PARSLEY, CHOPPED

¼ CUP GREEN PEPPER, CHOPPED

3 TABLESPOONS OLIVE OIL

1 CUP RICE

1 LARGE TOMATO, PEELED AND CHOPPED

1½ CUPS WATER
    PEPPER TO TASTE

1 LEMON, CUT IN WEDGES

½ CUP CHOPPED PARSLEY

SAUTÉ ONIONS, GARLIC, ½ CUP PARSLEY AND GREEN PEPPER IN OIL.

# Seafood Casserole

WE'LL NEED CRAB MEAT AND SHRIMP.

1 POUND COOKED CRABMEAT
1 POUND COOKED SHRIMP
1 CUP MAYONNAISE
½ CUP CHOPPED GREEN PEPPER
¼ CUP CHOPPED ONION
1½ CUPS CHOPPED CELERY
½ TEASPOON SALT
1 TABLESPOON WORCESTERSHIRE SAUCE
2 CUPS COARSELY CRUSHED POTATO CHIPS
PAPRIKA

COMBINE ALL INGREDIENTS EXCEPT POTATO CHIPS AND PAPRIKA. PILE ON SCALLOP SHELLS OR PUT IN CASSEROLE.

TOP WITH POTATO CHIPS AND DUST WITH PAPRIKA. BAKE IN A 400° OVEN FOR 25 MINUTES.

IT GOES GREAT WITH CHILLED WHITE WINE!

# CAPTAIN COOK'S PRAWNS

- 5 LARGE PRAWNS PER PERSON
- ½ POUND BUTTER
- 4 SHALLOTS, MINCED
- 4 CLOVES GARLIC, MINCED
- 3 TABLESPOONS STEAK SAUCE
- 2 TABLESPOONS LEMON JUICE
- ½ TEASPOON SALT
- ½ TEASPOON PEPPER

PEEL PRAWNS LEAVING ON THE TAIL. SPLIT DOWN THE MIDDLE LEAVING SIDES ATTACHED AT TAIL. SPREAD BUTTERFLY STYLE ON A BUTTERED COOKIE SHEET, TAIL UP.

BEAT REMAINING INGREDIENTS TOGETHER UNTIL CREAMY AND HEAT GENTLY. BROIL PRAWNS IN HOT OVEN FOR 4-5 MINUTES UNTIL DONE. DO NOT OVERCOOK. SERVE ON BED OF RICE WITH SAUCE OVER ALL.

# FILLET OF SOLE PARMESAN

—·—

½  CUP BUTTER
1  CUP PARMESAN CHEESE, GRATED
4  SOLE FILLETS
   PEPPER
   LEMON WEDGES

SPREAD HALF THE BUTTER IN SHALLOW BAKING DISH. SPRINKLE WITH HALF OF CHEESE. ARRANGE FISH IN ONE LAYER IN DISH. DOT WITH REST OF BUTTER AND SPRINKLE WITH REMAINING CHEESE. BAKE IN A 400° OVEN FOR 15 MINUTES, BASTING TWICE. SERVE WITH GRINDINGS OF BLACK PEPPER AND LEMON WEDGES.

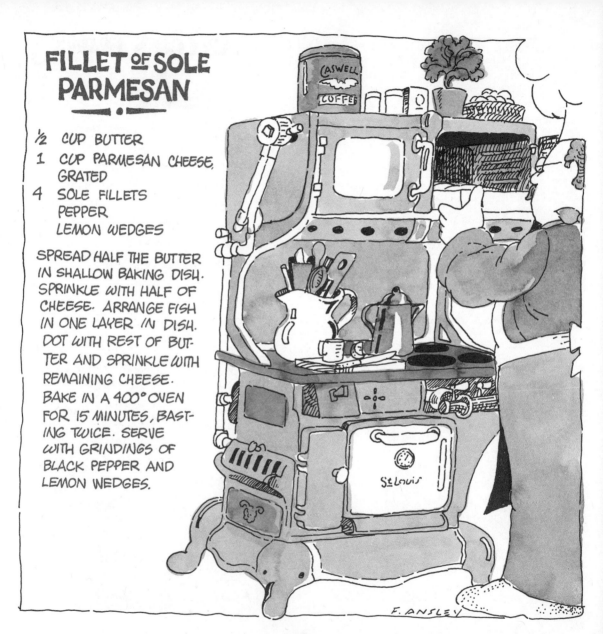

F. ANSLEY

NOW, WE MAKE **CHICKEN BREAST** WITH **PARMESAN CHEESE**

½ CHICKEN BREAST FOR EACH PERSON
⅓ CUP FLOUR
1 TABLESPOON SALT
¼ TEASPOON PEPPER
1 EGG, BEATEN
1 CUP BREAD CRUMBS
¼ CUP PARMESAN CHEESE, GRATED
3 TABLESPOONS BUTTER
3 TABLESPOONS OIL
LEMON WEDGES FOR GARNISH

POUND EACH PIECE OF CHICKEN BETWEEN WAXED PAPER TO ¼-INCH THICKNESS. SALT AND PEPPER EACH BREAST AND DIP FIRST INTO FLOUR THEN INTO EGG AND FINALLY INTO THE BREAD CRUMBS MIXED WITH THE PARMESAN CHEESE. SET ASIDE.

WHEN ALL PIECES ARE COATED, SAUTÉ IN BUTTER AND OIL UNTIL GOLDEN.

SERVE WITH LEMON WEDGES!

TODAY IS **CHICKEN CURRY**, SAHIB. FIRST WE TAKE 2 2½ POUND CHICKENS, DISJOINTED..

AND...

3 TABLESPOONS BUTTER
3 TABLESPOONS OIL
1 CUP DRY WHITE WINE
  SALT
  PEPPER
2 ONIONS, CHOPPED
1 TABLESPOON POWDERED GINGER
2 TABLESPOONS CURRY POWDER
3 EGG YOLKS
½ CUP CREAM

BROWN CHICKEN IN BUTTER AND OIL, RESERVING THE BACKS, NECKS AND GIBLETS. PUT BROWNED CHICKEN IN CASSEROLE WITH WINE. SEASON WITH SALT AND PEPPER.

COVER AND SIMMER FOR 1 HOUR. MAKE CHICKEN STOCK WITH 3 CUPS WATER, THE BACKS, NECKS AND GIBLETS. SIMMER WHILE CHICKEN IS COOKING.

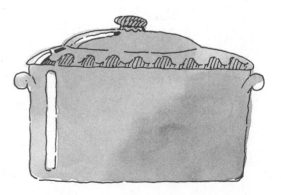

SAUTÉ ONIONS IN PAN USED TO BROWN CHICKEN. ADD GINGER, CURRY POWDER AND 3 CUPS CHICKEN STOCK. SIMMER 15 MINUTES.

BEAT EGG YOLKS AND ADD CREAM.

ADD THIS TO CURRY SAUCE AND HEAT GENTLY UNTIL SLIGHTLY THICKENED. DO NOT BOIL. POUR OVER CHICKEN AND SERVE WITH CONDIMENTS.

F. ANSLEY

## CHICKEN WITH ROSEMARY AND LEMON

| | |
|---|---|
| 1 | 3 POUND CHICKEN |
| 3 | TABLESPOONS BUTTER |
| 1 | TABLESPOON OIL |
| 1 | CLOVE GARLIC, MINCED |
| 1 | TABLESPOON FLOUR |
| 1½ | CUPS CHICKEN BROTH |
| | JUICE AND GRATED RIND OF 1 LARGE LEMON |
| ½ | TEASPOON ROSEMARY |
| ¼ | CUP DRY WHITE WINE |
| | SALT AND PEPPER |

CUT CHICKEN INTO SERVING PIECES AND BROWN IN BUTTER AND OIL. PUT CHICKEN IN A CASSEROLE. LIGHTLY BROWN THE GARLIC IN THE SAME PAN CHICKEN WAS BROWNED IN.

STIR IN THE FLOUR AND COOK FOR 2 MINUTES. REMOVE FROM HEAT AND WHISK IN THE CHICKEN BROTH.

# CAPTAIN COOK'S FRIED CHICKEN

1 3 POUND FRYING CHICKEN, DISJOINTED
1/3 CUP FLOUR
1 TABLESPOON SALT
1/4 TEASPOON PEPPER
SHORTENING

COMBINE FLOUR AND SEASONINGS IN PAPER BAG.

SHAKE CHICKEN PIECES IN BAG TO COAT AND SET ASIDE ON WAXED PAPER. HEAT ENOUGH SHORTENING TO COVER THE BOTTOM OF A HEAVY SKILLET WITH 1/4-INCH OF LIQUID AND COOK CHICKEN UNTIL BROWN AND CRISP..

.. AND THOROUGHLY DONE. DO NOT CROWD PAN.

EAT IT AT HOME OR TAKE IT TO A PICNIC!

# STAURANT

## LAMB SHANKS AND LENTILS

- 1½ CUPS LENTILS, SOAK OVERNIGHT
- 1 ONION STUCK WITH 2 WHOLE CLOVES
- 1 BAY LEAF
  SALT AND PEPPER
- 6 LAMB SHANKS
  FLOUR FOR DREDGING
- 3 TABLESPOONS OIL
- 1 CUP BEEF BOUILLON
- 1 MEDIUM ONION CHOPPED

HMM.. COOK LENTILS IN SALTED WATER WITH ONION AND BAY LEAF FOR 30 MINUTES. SET ASIDE. SALT, PEPPER AND FLOUR LAMB SHANKS AND BROWN IN OIL. REMOVE TO A CASSEROLE AND ADD BOUILLON. BRING TO BOIL, COVER AND SIMMER FOR 1½ HOURS.

DRAIN LENTILS AND DISCARD THE ONION. ARRANGE LENTILS IN FLAT OVEN-PROOF SERVING DISH AND TOP WITH LAMB SHANKS.

DEGREASE SAUCE IN WHICH SHANKS WERE COOKED AND POUR IT OVER LAMB AND LENTILS. SPRINKLE WITH CHOPPED ONION. BAKE, UNCOVERED, IN A 375° OVEN FOR 40 MINUTES.

HE'S GOT **SOMETHIN'** ON HIS MIND.

# Lamb Stew

## You'll Need:

- 3 pounds lean boneless lamb shoulder cut into 1½-inch pieces
- ¼ cup oil
- ¼ cup flour
- 1 teaspoon salt
- 1 teaspoon thyme
- ¼ teaspoon pepper
- 2 pounds potatoes, peeled and cut into ¼-inch slices
- 1 pound carrots, peeled and cut into ½-inch rounds
- 1 pound onions, peeled and sliced
- 4 cups chicken broth
- ¼ cup parsley, chopped

SAUTÉ LAMB IN OIL FOR 5 MINUTES. COMBINE FLOUR, SALT, THYME AND PEPPER.

SPRINKLE OVER THE LAMB AND SAUTÉ 5 MINUTES MORE.

ARRANGE A LAYER OF THE VEGETABLES IN A LARGE CASSEROLE AND PUT HALF THE LAMB OVER THE VEGETABLES AND CONTINUE LAYERING, ENDING WITH A LAYER OF VEGETABLES.

BRING CHICKEN BROTH TO A BOIL AND POUR OVER THE MEAT AND VEGETABLES.

NOW HE'S DOING JUST THAT.

COVER AND COOK IN A 300° OVEN FOR 2½ HOURS

SPRINKLE WITH PARSLEY AND SERVE.

# LAMB CURRY

3 POUNDS LAMB SHOULDER CUT IN 1-INCH PIECES
SALT AND PEPPER
3 TABLESPOONS OIL
2 ONIONS, CHOPPED

2 CUPS BOILING WATER
1 TABLESPOON FLOUR
2 TABLESPOONS CURRY POWDER

SEASON LAMB WITH SALT AND PEPPER AND BROWN IN OIL. REMOVE LAMB AND SAUTÉ ONIONS UNTIL LIMP.

RETURN LAMB AND ADD BOILING WATER, COVER, SIMMER 30 MINUTES.

MAKE A PASTE WITH ¼ CUP COLD WATER AND FLOUR. ADD THIS TO SAUCE, A LITTLE AT A TIME.

45

# CAPTAIN COOK'S BEST MEAT LOAF

## MEAT LOAF

¼ cup chopped onion
2 tablespoons butter
½ cup herb-seasoned stuffing
½ cup beef bouillon
1 pound ground chuck
1 tablespoon chopped parsley
3 tablespoons grated Parmesan cheese
1 egg, lightly beaten
1 teaspoon salt
¼ teaspoon pepper
1 8-oz. can tomato sauce
1 teaspoon oregano

SAUTÉ ONION IN BUTTER UNTIL LIMP. IN A LARGE BOWL, COMBINE STUFFING AND BROTH. ADD ONIONS AND ALL BUT LAST 2 INGREDIENTS. MIX LIGHTLY AND SHAPE INTO A LOAF.

PUT LOAF IN A SHALLOW BAKING PAN. BAKE IN A 375° OVEN FOR 30 MINUTES. POUR OVER TOMATO SAUCE AND SPRINKLE WITH OREGANO. BAKE 30 MINUTES MORE.

TASTE FOR PLEASURE!

# SWISS STEAK

2 POUNDS ROUND STEAK
  SALT AND PEPPER
  FLOUR FOR DREDGING
3 TABLESPOONS OIL
1 10½-OZ. CAN CREAM OF
  MUSHROOM SOUP
1 CUP MILK

CUT MEAT INTO SERVING SIZE PIECES AND PRESS FLOUR SEASONED WITH SALT AND PEPPER INTO EACH PIECE, USING THE EDGE OF A PLATE. BROWN STEAK IN OIL AND TRANSFER TO A CASSEROLE

REMOVE GREASE FROM PAN AND ADD SOUP AND MILK. BRING TO A BOIL, STIRRING. POUR OVER STEAK AND COVER. BAKE IN A 350° OVEN FOR 2 HOURS. SERVE WITH BAKED POTATOES.

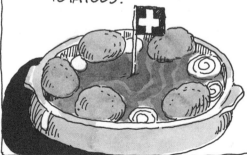

3½ lb. CHUCK ROAST
2 TBSP. OIL
2 TBSP. BUTTER
SALT & PEPPER
TO TASTE
2 ONIONS, CHOPPED
2 TBSP. DARK
CORN SYRUP
3 WHOLE
ANCHOVIES
16 WHOLE
PEPPERCORNS

16 WHOLE ALLSPICE
2 BAY LEAVES
2 10½ OZ. CANS
BOUILLON
1 CAN WATER
1 CAN RED WINE
1½ TSP. ARROW-
ROOT
¼ CUP COLD
WATER

SALT AND PEPPER CHUCK ROAST,
DREDGE WITH FLOUR, BROWN IN OIL
AND BUTTER. COMBINE ONIONS,
SYRUP, ANCHOVIES, PEPPERCORNS,
ALLSPICE, BAY LEAVES,
BOUILLON AND
WATER IN A
HEAVY ROAST-
ING PAN.

BRING TO BOIL,
ADD POT ROAST,
COVER AND SIMMER
FOR 3 HOURS.

48

49

## COME AN' GIT IT...
# SHORT RIBS OF BEEF!

3 TABLESPOONS OIL
1 MEDIUM ONION, CHOPPED
1 LARGE CLOVE GARLIC, CHOPPED
2 STALKS CELERY, CHOPPED
½ TEASPOON THYME
½ TEASPOON ROSEMARY
3½ POUNDS SHORT RIBS, CUT INTO SERVING PIECES
SALT AND PEPPER
FLOUR FOR DREDGING
1½ CUPS HOT BEEF BOUILLON

HEAT OIL IN LARGE SKILLET AND SAUTÉ UNTIL LIMP, ONION, GARLIC AND CELERY SEASONED WITH THYME AND ROSEMARY. TRANSFER TO CASSEROLE.

IN SAME SKILLET BROWN SHORT RIBS THAT HAVE BEEN DREDGED IN SEASONED FLOUR.

ADD RIBS TO CASSEROLE AND POUR OVER HOT BOUILLON.

BRING TO BOIL, COVER AND BAKE IN A 300° OVEN FOR 2 HOURS.

SKIM OFF FAT AND THICKEN SAUCE WITH SEASONED FLOUR MIXED WITH A LITTLE COLD WATER. BRING TO SIMMER AND COOK ANOTHER 10 MINUTES.

HERE THEY COME!

# BRAISED ★OXTAILS

**GIT:**

3 POUNDS OXTAILS, DISJOINTED
SALT & PEPPER
FLOUR FOR DREDGING
3 TABLESPOONS OIL
1 CUP CARROTS, DICED
1 CLOVE GARLIC, MINCED
12 SMALL WHITE ONIONS, PEELED
2 CUPS DRY RED WINE
1 BAY LEAF
½ TEASPOON THYME
BOUILLON
1 CUP MUSHROOMS
½ CUP CHOPPED PARSLEY

REMOVE AS MUCH FAT AS POSSIBLE FROM OXTAILS. SALT, PEPPER AND ROLL THEM IN FLOUR, PODNER!

FLOUR
XXX

BROWN OXTAILS IN OIL AND REMOVE TO CASSEROLE. BROWN THE CARROTS, GARLIC AND ONIONS IN SAUTÉ PAN AND ADD TO CASSEROLE ALONG WITH WINE AND SEASONINGS.

ADD BOUILLON TO BARELY COVER AND BRING TO BOIL. COVER AND PUT IN A 350° OVEN FOR 2½ HOURS.

BROWN MUSHROOMS IN SAUTÉ PAN.

REMOVE EXCESS FAT FROM CASSEROLE AND ADD MUSHROOMS.
REHEAT GENTLY AND SERVE WITH PARSLEY SPRINKLED OVER ALL.

ADD CARROTS, CHICKEN BROTH, BAY LEAF AND SEASONINGS. MIX FLOUR WITH A LITTLE BUTTER AND ADD IT TO THE BROTH, STIRRING UNTIL SMOOTH AND THICKENED.

POUR OVER VEAL. COVER AND BAKE IN A 350° OVEN FOR 1 HOUR.

SAUTÉ THE MUSHROOMS IN 4 TABLESPOONS BUTTER UNTIL GOLDEN AND ADD THEM TO THE CASSEROLE WITH THE PEAS AND CREAM.

F. ANSLEY

BAKE UNCOVERED FOR 20 MINUTES.

BON..

..APPETIT!

55

# MACARONI AND CHEESE

AN OLD FAVORITE!

½ LB. MACARONI
3 TABLESPOONS BUTTER
3 TABLESPOONS FLOUR
1½ CUPS MILK
1 TEASPOON SALT
½ TEASPOON DRY MUSTARD
HOT PEPPER SAUCE TO TASTE
1½ CUPS GRATED CHEESE
BUTTERED BREAD CRUMBS

COOK MACARONI IN SALTED WATER UNTIL JUST TENDER.

MAKE A WHITE SAUCE BY MELTING THE BUTTER AND BLENDING IN THE FLOUR. COOK GENTLY FOR 2 MINUTES.

HEAT THE MILK AND POUR IT INTO THE BUTTER-FLOUR MIXTURE.

STIR WITH A WHISK AND COOK UNTIL THICK. ADD SEASONINGS AND COOK FOR 5 MINUTES.

BUTTER A 2-QUART BAKING DISH AND ARRANGE ALTERNATE LAYERS OF MACARONI, SAUCE AND CHEESE.

COVER THE TOP WITH BUTTERED BREAD CRUMBS AND BAKE IN A 350° OVEN FOR 30 MINUTES OR UNTIL GOLDEN.

LOOKS GOLDEN TO ME.

LET'S EAT!

F. ansley

MOSTACCIOLI WITH FOUR CHEESES...

..AND ASPARAGUS!

1 CUP ASPARAGUS TIPS
2-OZ. GRUYÈRE CHEESE, GRATED
2-OZ. FONTINELLA CHEESE GRATED
2-OZ. PARMESAN CHEESE, GRATED
1 CUP CREAM, SCALDED
1 16-OZ. PACKAGE MOSTACCIOLI
2-OZ. MOZZARELLA CHEESE, GRATED

COOK ASPARAGUS TIPS UNTIL BARELY TENDER, DRAIN. ADD FIRST THREE CHEESES TO SCALDED CREAM. COOK MOSTACCIOLI ACCORDING TO DIRECTIONS ON PACKAGE, DRAIN. IN HEATED BOWL, MIX CREAM-CHEESE MIXTURE WITH MOSTACCIOLI, ASPARAGUS AND MOZZARELLA CHEESE.

SERVE WITH GENEROUS GRINDINGS OF BLACK PEPPER.

# PASTA WITH BUTTER AND CHEESE

ALL YOU NEED IS:

1 POUND PACKAGE SPAGHETTI OR OTHER PASTA

¼ POUND BUTTER CUT IN SMALL PIECES

1 CUP PARMESAN CHEESE, GRATED

BLACK PEPPER

COOK PASTA ACCORDING TO DIRECTIONS ON PACKAGE, DRAIN. MIX IN WARM BOWL WITH BUTTER AND CHEESE. SERVE WITH GENEROUS GRINDINGS OF BLACK PEPPER.

SO SIMPLE YET SO GOOD!

IF YOU GATHER:

- ½ POUND MUSHROOMS, SLICED
- 3 TABLESPOONS BUTTER
- ½ POUND PROSCIUTTO, DICED
- 1 POUND PACKAGE SPAGHETTI
- 2 TABLESPOONS CREAM PARMESAN CHEESE, GRATED
- BLACK PEPPER

WE CAN MAKE A DELICIOUS **PASTA WITH PROSCIUTTO AND MUSHROOMS!**

COOK SPAGHETTI ACCORDING TO DIRECTIONS ON PACKAGE, DRAIN.

SAUTE MUSHROOMS IN BUTTER FOR 5 MINUTES, ADD PROSCIUTTO.

IN A WARM BOWL, TOSS SPAGHETTI WITH CREAM, ADD PROSCIUTTO AND MUSHROOMS. SERVE WITH PARMESAN CHEESE AND GENEROUS GRINDINGS OF BLACK PEPPER.

## SPAGHETTI WITH CLAM SAUCE

3 CLOVES GARLIC, MINCED
1/3 CUP OLIVE OIL
2 7oz. CANS MINCED CLAMS
1/2 CUP PARSLEY, CHOPPED
1 POUND PACKAGE SPAGHETTI
BLACK PEPPER

SAUTÉ GARLIC IN 1/2 OF OLIVE OIL UNTIL LIMP. DO NOT BROWN. ADD REST OF OIL AND JUICE FROM CLAMS, 1/2 OF PARSLEY AND BRING TO SIMMER. ADD CLAMS AND HEAT ONLY.

COOK SPAGHETTI AC-CORDING TO DIRECTIONS ON PACKAGE, DRAIN. IN HEATED BOWL MIX SPAGHETTI WITH CLAMS AND REST OF PARSLEY. SERVE WITH GENEROUS GRINDINGS OF BLACK PEPPER.

·SPAGHETTI ALLA CARBONARA·

((COAL MINER'S WIFE'S SPAGHETTI))

2  WHOLE EGGS
2  EGG YOLKS
1  CUP GRATED PARMESAN CHEESE
8  SLICES BACON, DICED
1  TEASPOON DRIED RED PEPPER
   FLAKES
½ CUP CREAM
1  POUND PACKAGE SPAGHETTI
4  TABLESPOONS BUTTER
   SALT AND PEPPER

**B**EAT EGGS AND EGG YOLKS TOGETHER WITH ½ CUP CHEESE, SET ASIDE. FRY BACON UNTIL CRISP.

**R**EMOVE FROM PAN ALL BUT FOUR TABLESPOONS BACON FAT AND ADD THE PEPPER FLAKES AND CREAM. BRING TO SIMMER.

COOK SPAGHETTI ACCORDING TO DIRECTIONS ON PACKAGE & DRAIN.

IN A LARGE, HEATED BOWL, COMBINE SPAGHETTI, BUTTER, CREAM-BACON AND EGG MIXTURE.

PASTA

MIX GENTLY. TASTE FOR SALT. SERVE WITH REMAINING CHEESE AND FRESHLY GROUND PEPPER.

PASTA

IT'S GREAT AFTER A HARD DAY IN THE MINES.

CAN YOU DIG IT?

O MIO SOLE..

NOW HE'S MAKING **SPAGHETTI** WITH **GARLIC AND OIL!**

1  POUND PACKAGE SPAGHETTI
2  TEASPOONS MINCED GARLIC
2  TEASPOONS SALT
½  CUP OLIVE OIL
¼  CUP CHOPPED PARSLEY
   BLACK PEPPER

COOK SPAGHETTI ACCORDING TO DIRECTIONS ON PACKAGE. WHILE SPAGHETTI IS COOKING, SAUTÉ GARLIC WITH SALT IN OLIVE OIL UNTIL GOLDEN. DO NOT BROWN. WHEN SPAGHETTI IS COOKED, DRAIN AND MIX IN HEATED BOWL WITH GARLIC AND OIL.

SPRINKLE WITH PARSLEY AND SERVE WITH GENEROUS GRINDINGS OF BLACK PEPPER.

HOW DOES HE DO IT?

# TO MAKE A NICE **TOMATO SAUCE**
## **FOR PASTA**

YOU'LL NEED:

- 4 CLOVES GARLIC, CUT IN HALF
- 1 SMALL ONION, SLICED
- 2 TABLESPOONS OLIVE OIL
- 1 16 oz. CAN PLUM TOMATOES, BLENDED
- ¼ TEASPOON BASIL
- ¼ TEASPOON OREGANO
- ½ CUP CHOPPED PARSLEY
   ROMANO CHEESE, GRATED
   RED PEPPER FLAKES

SAUTÉ ONION AND GARLIC IN OIL UNTIL ONIONS ARE TRANSPARENT. DISCARD GARLIC. ADD TOMATOES AND SEASONINGS AND SIMMER FOR 15 MINUTES.

SERVE OVER COOKED PASTA AND SPRINKLE WITH PARSLEY, CHEESE AND PEPPER FLAKES.

Mama Mia!

THEY'RE LITTLE WHEELS.

## ● TORTELLINI WITH HAM AND PEAS

1 16-oz. PACKAGE FROZEN TORTELLINI

4 SLICES BOILED HAM, DICED

3 TABLESPOONS BUTTER

1 CUP CREAM

1 CUP COOKED PEAS

½ CUP GRATED PARMESAN CHEESE

COOK TORTELLINI ACCORDING TO DIRECTIONS ON PACKAGE. WHILE TORTELLINI ARE COOKING, SAUTÉ HAM IN BUTTER FOR 5 MINUTES.

ADD CREAM AND SIMMER UNTIL TORTELLINI ARE COOKED. DRAIN TORTELLINI AND ADD TO CREAM AND HAM.

ADD PEAS AND TOSS WITH PARMESAN CHEESE. SERVE WITH GENEROUS GRINDINGS OF BLACK PEPPER.

DELIZIOSO!

MANGIA BENE!

## CHILI WITH BEANS

3 TABLESPOONS OIL
1 LARGE ONION, CHOPPED
2 CLOVES GARLIC, CHOPPED
1 POUND GROUND CHUCK
1½ CUPS CANNED TOMATOES
1 GREEN PEPPER, CHOPPED
1½ TEASPOON SALT
¼ TEASPOON BASIL
½ TEASPOON CELERY SEED
¼ TEASPOON CAYENNE
1 BAY LEAF
1 TEASPOON CUMIN SEED, CRUSHED
2 TABLESPOONS CHILI POWDER
3 CUPS WATER
1 16 OZ. CAN KIDNEY BEANS, DRAINED

SAUTÉ THE ONION AND GARLIC IN OIL UNTIL GOLDEN. ADD MEAT AND BROWN. PLACE IN A LARGE PAN AND ADD ALL OTHER INGREDIENTS EXCEPT BEANS.

BRING TO BOIL AND SIMMER FOR THREE HOURS, UNCOVERED. ADD THE BEANS, HEAT AND SERVE.

F. ANSLEY

FER COWBOY STEW:

1 CUP NAVY BEANS, SOAKED OVERNIGHT.
3 LARGE ONIONS, CHOPPED
2 TABLESPOONS BUTTER
1 POUND GROUND BEEF
1 16-OZ. CAN TOMATOES
1 TEASPOON SALT
2 TABLESPOONS BROWN SUGAR
1½ TEASPOONS DRY MUSTARD
4 STRIPS BACON, COOKED CRISP & CRUMBLED

COOK BEANS IN SALTED WATER FOR 1 HOUR, DRAIN. IN A LARGE SKILLET SAUTÉ ONIONS IN BUTTER UNTIL TRANSPARENT.

ADD BEEF AND BROWN.

ADD TOMATOES, BREAKING THEM UP WITH A FORK. ADD SEASONINGS AND BEANS. HEAT THOROUGHLY. SERVE WITH BACON SPRINKLED ON TOP.

# FAIRY PUDDING

6 OZ. MEDIUM EGG NOODLES

1 10½-OZ. CAN CREAM OF MUSHROOM SOUP

1 CUP MILK

1 6½-OZ. CAN TUNA, DRAINED

1 CUP CHEDDAR CHEESE GRATED

1 2½-OZ. CAN SLICED MUSHROOMS

¼ CUP SLICED STUFFED GREEN OLIVES

CRUSHED POTATO CHIPS

COOK NOODLES ACCORDING TO DIRECTIONS ON PACKAGE. DRAIN. COMBINE SOUP, MILK AND TUNA AND BRING TO A BOIL. STIR IN COOKED NOODLES, CHEESE, MUSHROOMS AND OLIVES.

EGG NOODLES

POUR INTO A BUTTERED CASSEROLE AND TOP WITH POTATO CHIPS. BAKE IN A 375° OVEN FOR 15-20 MINUTES.

THE PUDDING FAIRY WAS HERE.

F. ANSLEY

69

TO MAKE **EGGPLANT CASSEROLE**

TAKE ONE LARGE EGGPLANT..

~AND~
SALT AND PEPPER
1 EGG, BEATEN
  FLOUR
4 TABLESPOONS
  OLIVE OIL
½ POUND TELEME CHEESE
1 8oz. CAN TOMATO
  SAUCE
½ TEASPOON MARJORAM
1 TABLESPOON DRY
  SHERRY WINE

SLICE EGGPLANT INTO 3/4 INCH SLICES...

SALT AND PEPPER EACH SLICE AND DIP INTO BEATEN EGG. DUST WITH FLOUR AND SAUTÉ IN OIL UNTIL BROWNED.

LAYER EGGPLANT IN CASSEROLE WITH SLICES OF TELEME CHEESE...

IN SAUTE' PAN ADD TOMATO SAUCE, MARJORAM, SHERRY AND SALT AND PEPPER TO TASTE.

BRING TO BOIL AND POUR OVER EGGPLANT. COVER AND BAKE AT 325° FOR 45 MINUTES.

REMOVE COVER AND BASTE. COOK 15 MINUTES MORE, UNCOVERED.

## HAM AND BEAN CASSEROLE..

WHY NOT?

Will Need:
2 large onions, chopped
3 tablespoons butter
1 large ham slice, cut into ½-inch cubes
2 tablespoons flour
1 cup consommé
1 cup red wine
2 16-oz. cans kidney beans, drained
1 cup Cheddar cheese, grated

SAUTÉ ONIONS IN BUTTER UNTIL TRANSPARENT. ADD HAM CUBES AND SPRINKLE WITH FLOUR. COOK FOR 5 MINUTES. ADD CONSOMMÉ, RED WINE AND KIDNEY BEANS.

MIX THOROUGHLY AND PLACE IN A CASSEROLE. BAKE, UNCOVERED, IN A 350° OVEN FOR 30 MINUTES. COVER TOP WITH GRATED CHEESE AND BAKE FOR 15 MINUTES MORE.

HOT STUFF!

# Joe's SPECIAL WITH ZUCCHINI

**·INGREDIENTI:**

1 POUND GROUND CHUCK
1 ONION, CHOPPED
4 SMALL ZUCCHINI, SLICED
  SALT AND PEPPER
1 TEASPOON OREGANO
6 EGGS, BEATEN

SERVE WITH PARMESAN CHEESE.

BROWN THE MEAT AND ONION IN A LARGE SKILLET, BREAKING UP THE MEAT AS IT BROWNS. ADD THE ZUCCHINI AND COOK 5 MINUTES MORE. ADD SALT AND PEPPER TO TASTE AND OREGANO. ADD EGGS AND COOK SLOWLY WHILE STIRRING GENTLY UNTIL EGGS ARE DONE.

F. ANSLEY

LOOKS LIKE YOU'RE GONNA MAKE **HAM HOCKS** AND **LIMA BEANS!**

ONE OF MY FAVORITES

SOAK 1 POUND DRY LIMA BEANS OVERNIGHT.

PLACE 2½ POUNDS HAM HOCKS, 1 LARGE ONION, SLICED, IN A LARGE KETTLE WITH 2 QUARTS OF WATER.

BRING TO A BOIL, COVER, AND SIMMER FOR 1½ HOURS.

ADD DRAINED LIMAS, 3 TABLESPOONS BROWN SUGAR, 1 TABLESPOON WORCESTERSHIRE SAUCE, ½ TEASPOON SALT AND 1 TEASPOON DRY MUSTARD AND SIMMER ANOTHER HOUR, COVERED.

REMOVE HAM HOCKS AND SHRED THE MEAT. RETURN TO POT AND TASTE FOR SEASONINGS.

THEN *FEED* THAT HUNGRY CREW!

LETS EAT!

## MACARONI WITH SAUSAGES

### C. COOK — TAKE 1

 **STARRING:**

- 1 8 OZ. PACKAGE ELBOW MACARONI
- ½ ONION, CHOPPED
- 2 TABLESPOONS BUTTER
- 1 TEASPOON DRY MUSTARD
- 1 TEASPOON WORCESTERSHIRE SAUCE
- 1 TABLESPOON FLOUR
- 1 TEASPOON SALT
- ¼ TEASPOON PEPPER
- 2½ CUPS MILK
- 2 CUPS SHARP CHEDDAR CHEESE, GRATED
- 1 POUND LINK SAUSAGES
- ¼ CUP PARMESAN CHEESE, GRATED

**SCENE 1**

COOK MACARONI ACCORDING TO DIRECTIONS AND DRAIN. SAUTÉ ONION IN BUTTER UNTIL SOFT, ADD MUSTARD, WORCESTERSHIRE SAUCE, FLOUR, SALT AND PEPPER.

**SCENE 2**

COOK FOR 2 MINUTES STIRRING. ADD MILK STIRRING CONSTANTLY. SIMMER 2 MINUTES.

IT'S A STIRRING SCENE!

**SCENE 3**

REMOVE FROM HEAT AND ADD 1 CUP CHEDDAR CHEESE. STIR UNTIL CHEESE MELTS. ADD MACARONI.

**SCENE 4**

BROWN SAUSAGES AND DRAIN. IN A CASSEROLE PUT A LAYER OF MACARONI AND SAUSAGES AND SPRINKLE WITH HALF THE REMAINING CHEDDAR CHEESE AND PARMESAN.

**SCENE 5**

LAYER THE REST OF THE MACARONI AND SAUSAGES AND SPRINKLE WITH REST OF CHEESES. BAKE IN A 375° OVEN FOR 45 MINUTES.

**FINALE!**

F. Ainsley

LET'S MAKE **PORK CHOPS AND RICE.**

4 THICK PORK CHOPS
1 CLOVE GARLIC
3 TABLESPOONS OIL
2 LARGE ONIONS, SLICED
1½ CUPS RICE
3 CUPS CHICKEN BROTH
¼ TEASPOON POWDERED THYME
SALT AND PEPPER TO TASTE

RUB CHOPS WITH GARLIC AND BROWN THEM IN OIL. PUT CHOPS IN CASSEROLE. SAUTÉ ONIONS IN SAME OIL UNTIL TRANSPARENT. PUT ONIONS ON CHOPS AND ADD RICE. HEAT CHICKEN BROTH IN SAUTÉ PAN WITH SEASONINGS AND POUR OVER CHOPS.

COVER AND BAKE IN A 350° OVEN FOR 45 MINUTES.

# RICE WITH ORANGE AND RAISINS

1 cup uncooked long grain rice

½ cube butter

½ cup sour cream

2 teaspoons grated orange rind

½ cup golden raisins plumped in orange juice, drained

Chopped parsley

F. ANSLEY

**C**OOK RICE ACCORDING TO DIRECTIONS ON PACKAGE AND MIX THOROUGHLY WITH BUTTER, SOUR CREAM, ORANGE RIND AND RAISINS.

**P**UT IN AN OVENPROOF DISH AND BAKE IN A 300° OVEN FOR 20 MINUTES OR UNTIL HOT.

**S**PRINKLE WITH PARSLEY AND SERVE.

# SAUSAGES WITH MASHED POTATOES

| | |
|---|---|
| 2-4 | SAUSAGES FOR EACH PERSON |
| 1 | 10½-OZ. CAN CONSOMMÉ |
| 1 | CAN WHITE WINE |
| 1 | CARROT, PEELED AND CHOPPED |
| 1 | STALK CELERY, CHOPPED |
| 4 | LARGE POTATOES |
| | HOT MILK |

PRICK SAUSAGES AND BROWN TO RELEASE FAT. IN A SAUCE PAN, COMBINE THE CONSOMMÉ, WINE, CARROT AND CELERY.

SIMMER FOR 15 MINUTES.

ADD SAUSAGES AND SIMMER 20 MINUTES MORE.

COOK AND MASH THE POTATOES, ADDING JUST ENOUGH HOT MILK TO MAKE DRY MASHED POTATOES. MOUND POTATOES ON INDIVIDUAL SOUP PLATES AND ARRANGE SAUSAGES ON TOP. POUR SAUCE OVER AND SERVE.

# AMAZING ZUCCHINI CASSEROLE!

THE GREAT ZUCCHINI!!

2 pounds zucchini, sliced in ¼ inch rounds

2 eggs, lightly beaten

½ cup bread crumbs

¼ cup olive oil

2 cloves garlic, mashed

9 tablespoons Parmesan cheese, grated

salt and pepper to taste

SIMMER ZUCCHINI IN SALTED WATER FOR 10 MINUTES. DRAIN THOROUGHLY, PLACE IN A CASSEROLE AND MASH COARSELY WITH A FORK. ADD BEATEN EGGS, BREAD CRUMBS, OLIVE OIL, GARLIC AND 6 TABLESPOONS PARMESAN CHEESE. SALT AND PEPPER TO TASTE. SPRINKLE TOP WITH 3 TABLESPOONS PARMESAN CHEESE. BAKE UNCOVERED IN A 350° OVEN FOR 45 MINUTES.

AMAZING!

J. ANSLEY

IF YOU ALL FANCY SOME
## SPOON BREAD
THEN FETCH:
- 1 CUP MILK
- ½ CUP YELLOW CORNMEAL
- ½ TEASPOON SALT
- 3 TABLESPOONS BUTTER
- 3 EGG YOLKS
- 3 EGG WHITES

HEAT MILK UNTIL SMALL BUBBLES FORM AROUND THE SIDE OF THE PAN. SLOWLY POUR IN THE CORNMEAL, STIRRING CONSTANTLY. COOK, WITHOUT BOILING, UNTIL THICK AND SMOOTH.

ADD SALT AND BUTTER AND STIR UNTIL BUTTER IS ABSORBED.

REMOVE FROM HEAT
AND ADD EGG YOLKS
ONE AT A TIME,
BEATING AFTER EACH
ADDITION. BEAT THE
EGG WHITES UNTIL
THEY FORM
STIFF PEAKS.

GENTLY FOLD A
LARGE SPOONFUL OF
EGG WHITE INTO THE
CORNMEAL MIXTURE.
THEN GENTLY, BUT
THOROUGHLY, FOLD
IN THE REST.

POUR INTO A LARGE
BUTTERED SOUFFLÉ OR
BAKING DISH AND BAKE
IN A 375° OVEN
FOR 35 MINUTES OR
UNTIL GOLDEN.

THEN ENJOY YO' SPOON BREAD
ON THE VERANDAH!..

# TAMALE PIE

| | |
|---|---|
| 3 | TABLESPOONS BUTTER |
| 3 | TABLESPOONS OIL |
| 1 | SMALL ONION, CHOPPED |
| 1 | CLOVE GARLIC, MINCED |
| 1 | POUND GROUND BEEF |
| ½ | POUND PORK SAUSAGE |
| 1 | 16 OZ. CAN TOMATOES |
| 1 | 8¾ OZ. CAN WHOLE KERNEL CORN |
| 2 | TEASPOONS SALT |
| 2 | TEASPOONS CHILI POWDER |
| 24 | PITTED RIPE OLIVES |
| 1 | CUP CORN MEAL |
| 1 | CUP MILK |
| 2 | EGGS, BEATEN |
| 1½ | CUPS GRATED CHEDDAR CHEESE |

HEAT OIL AND BUTTER IN A FRYING PAN AND SAUTÉ ONION AND GARLIC UNTIL GOLDEN. ADD GROUND BEEF AND SAUSAGE AND BROWN.

Put tomatoes, corn, salt and chili powder in a saucepan and simmer 20 minutes.

Combine with meat and pour into a shallow pan, 10 x 14 inches. Press olives into mixture.

Combine cornmeal, milk, eggs and spread over filling. Sprinkle with cheese.

Bake for 1 hour in a 350° oven.

I wish Speedy Gonzales was doin' the cooking..

ANSLEY

**WINE CHEESE PUFF!**

8 SLICES WHITE BREAD, TRIMMED OF CRUSTS
¼ POUND SOFTENED BUTTER
1 POUND CHEDDAR CHEESE, GRATED
8 EGGS
2½ CUPS MILK
½ CUP DRY SHERRY WINE
1 TABLESPOON DRY MUSTARD
2 TABLESPOONS BEAU MONDE SEASONING
2 TABLESPOONS WORCESTERSHIRE SAUCE
HOT SAUCE TO TASTE

BUTTER BOTH SIDES OF BREAD SLICES AND LAYER THEM AND THE CHEESE IN A CASSEROLE. MIX EGGS, MILK, SHERRY, DRY MUSTARD, BEAU MONDE, WORCESTERSHIRE SAUCE AND HOT PEPPER SAUCE. POUR OVER BREAD AND CHEESE.

COVER AND REFRIGERATE OVERNIGHT. BRING TO ROOM TEMPERATURE AND BAKE, UNCOVERED IN A 350° OVEN FOR 1 HOUR.

TEST WITH SILVER KNIFE FOR DONENESS.

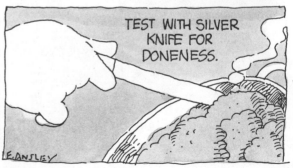

E. ANSLEY

# TO MAKE FANTASTIC

**YOU'LL NEED:**

- 5 16-oz. CANS PORK AND BEANS
- 2 CUPS DRY WHITE WINE
- 1 CUP DARK BROWN SUGAR
- 1 CUP ORANGE HONEY
- 1 TABLESPOON CRUMBLED BAY LEAF
- 1 TABLESPOON FRESHLY GROUND BLACK PEPPER

MIX ALL INGREDIENTS AND PUT INTO A BEAN POT, COVER. COOK IN A SLOW OVEN, 300° FOR 3 HOURS. CHECK OCCASIONALLY TO SEE IF LIQUID IS GONE. IF TOO DRY ADD MORE WINE AND COOK DOWN.

THANKS, OLD BEAN.

**BEANS BRETONNE**

1½ CUPS SMALL WHITE BEANS
1 CUP STEWED TOMATOES
1 CUP CHICKEN BROTH
6 PIMENTOS
1 ONION, FINELY CHOPPED
2 CLOVES GARLIC, FINELY CHOPPED
4 TABLESPOONS BUTTER
2 TEASPOONS SALT

SOAK BEANS OVERNIGHT IN 6 CUPS WATER. DRAIN, ADD FRESH WATER AND SIMMER FOR 1 HOUR OR UNTIL SOFT. PUT TOMATOES AND PIMENTOS THROUGH A FOOD MILL.

SAUTÉ ONION AND GARLIC IN 2 TABLESPOONS OF THE BUTTER. COMBINE DRAINED BEANS AND REST OF INGREDIENTS IN A CASSEROLE.

COVER AND BAKE AT 250° FOR 2 HOURS OR UNTIL MOST OF THE LIQUID IS ABSORBED.

FORMIDABLE!

F. ANSLEY

TO MAKE
**CORN OYSTERS**
WE NEED 1 CUP CORN CUT FROM COB, 3 TO 4 MEDIUM COBS..

AND—
1 EGG YOLK
2 TABLESPOONS FLOUR
SALT AND PEPPER
1 EGG WHITE, BEATEN STIFF
OIL

COMBINE CORN, EGG YOLK, FLOUR AND SALT AND PEPPER TO TASTE.

FOLD IN BEATEN EGG WHITE. DROP BY SPOONFULS ONTO HOT GREASED SKILLET AND COOK 1 OR 2 MINUTES ON EACH SIDE UNTIL GOLDEN.

DRAIN ON PAPER TOWELS AND SPRINKLE WITH SALT.

KEEP WARM IN 200° OVEN UNTIL ALL ARE COOKED.

ENJOY!

TO MAKE A DELICIOUS **CARROT SALAD**
YOU'LL NEED:
5 MEDIUM CARROTS, GRATED
1 7-OZ. CAN CRUSHED
   PINEAPPLE, DRAINED
⅓ CUP SEEDLESS RAISINS
⅓ CUP WALNUT MEATS,
   BROKEN IN SMALL PIECES
   MAYONNAISE

COMBINE INGREDIENTS WITH
ENOUGH MAYONNAISE TO BIND.

TO MAKE AN
**APPLE SALAD**
TAKE:
3 LARGE, CRISP GREEN
   APPLES
2 CELERY STALKS,
   COARSELY CHOPPED
⅓ CUP WALNUT MEATS,
   BROKEN
   MAYONNAISE

PEEL APPLES AND
CUT INTO ½-INCH DICE.
COMBINE WITH CELERY
AND WALNUTS. BIND
WITH MAYONNAISE.

MAY

F. ANSLEY

91

LOOKS LIKE HE'S GONNA MAKE
## COLE SLAW

### ·RECIPE·

½ CABBAGE, CHOPPED
1 MEDIUM ONION, CHOPPED
3 TABLESPOONS WINE VINEGAR
1 CLOVE GARLIC, MASHED
½ TEASPOON DRY MUSTARD
¼ TEASPOON POWDERED THYME
½ TEASPOON SALT
½ TEASPOON PEPPER
1 TEASPOON BEAU MONDE SEASONING
MAYONNAISE

PLACE CABBAGE AND ONION IN BOWL.

MIX ALL OTHER INGREDIENTS EXCEPT MAYONNAISE AND DRESS CABBAGE.

MARINATE CABBAGE FOR ONE HOUR. MIX IN ENOUGH MAYONNAISE TO BIND. TASTE FOR SEASONINGS.

THEN TASTE!

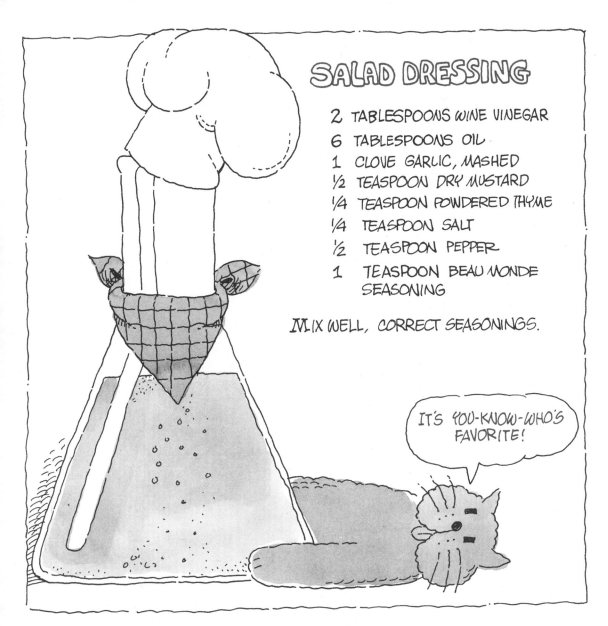

# SALAD DRESSING

2 TABLESPOONS WINE VINEGAR
6 TABLESPOONS OIL
1 CLOVE GARLIC, MASHED
½ TEASPOON DRY MUSTARD
¼ TEASPOON POWDERED THYME
¼ TEASPOON SALT
½ TEASPOON PEPPER
1 TEASPOON BEAU MONDE SEASONING

MIX WELL, CORRECT SEASONINGS.

IT'S YOU-KNOW-WHO'S FAVORITE!

# FOR OUR PICNIC, MY NICE
# SPECIAL POTATO SALAD

- 4 MEDIUM-LARGE POTATOES
- 1 MEDIUM ONION, CHOPPED
- 2 STALKS OF CELERY, CHOPPED
- 3 TABLESPOONS WINE VINEGAR
- 1 CLOVE GARLIC, MINCED
- ½ TEASPOON DRY MUSTARD
- ¼ TEASPOON POWDERED THYME
- ½ TEASPOON SALT
- ½ TEASPOON PEPPER
- 1 TEASPOON BEAU MONDE SEASONING
  MAYONNAISE
  CHOPPED PARSLEY

DON'T FORGET THE ANTS.

COOK PEELED AND QUARTERED POTATOES IN SALTED WATER UNTIL BARELY TENDER. DRAIN AND WHILE STILL HOT, CUT INTO MEDIUM-SMALL PIECES. COMBINE WITH ONION AND CELERY.

MAKE A DRESSING WITH REST OF INGREDIENTS EXCEPTING MAYONNAISE. DRESS POTATOES WHILE STILL WARM.

BEFORE SERVING, BIND WITH MAYONNAISE AND SPRINKLE WITH CHOPPED PARSLEY.

TO MAKE A

# SPECIAL DRESSING

YOU NEED:

- 3 SHALLOTS, MINCED
- 1 TABLESPOON DIJON MUSTARD
- 2 TABLESPOONS WINE VINEGAR
- 1 EGG YOLK
  SALT
  PEPPER
- 1 CUP OIL

PUT ALL INGREDIENTS, EXCEPT OIL, IN BOWL AND MIX. SLOWLY DRIBBLE IN OIL WHILE WHISKING. CONTINUE UNTIL OIL IS USED AND MIXTURE IS LIKE THIN MAYONNAISE.

USE ON SALAD GREENS OR ON VEGETABLES.

# SPINACH SALAD

2 BUNCHES OF SPINACH
2 EGGS, HARD BOILED AND SLICED
  SALT & PEPPER
6 BACON SLICES DICED AND FRIED CRISP
½ CUP BACON FAT
¼ CUP VINEGAR
2 TABLESPOONS LEMON JUICE
2 TEASPOONS SUGAR
½ TEASPOON WORCESTERSHIRE SAUCE

CLEAN SPINACH AND TEAR INTO BITE-SIZE PIECES. PLACE IN LARGE WARM BOWL WITH EGG SLICES ON TOP. SPRINKLE WITH SALT AND PEPPER.

HEAT REMAINING INGREDIENTS UNTIL VERY HOT AND POUR OVER SPINACH.

TOSS GENTLY AND SERVE ON WARM SALAD PLATES.

TOMATO·PEAR CHUTNEY

1 POUND TOMATOES, CHOPPED
1 POUND PEARS, PEELED AND CHOPPED
1 ONION, COARSELY CHOPPED
1/8 TEASPOON CAYENNE
1/2 TEASPOON DRY MUSTARD
1/2 TEASPOON GINGER
1 TEASPOON SALT
1/2 CUP VINEGAR
1 CUP SUGAR
1 GREEN PEPPER, CHOPPED
1 4-oz. CAN CHOPPED PIMIENTOS

WHO'S MAJOR GREY?

Mustard

MIX ALL INGREDIENTS EXCEPT PIMIENTO AND SIMMER FOR ONE HOUR, STIRRING OCCASIONALLY. ADD PIMIENTO AND COOK 5 MINUTES MORE.

PACK INTO JARS AND SEAL.

98

WE'LL NEED SOME NICE PEARS TO MAKE **PEAR CHUTNEY!**

5 POUNDS FIRM PEARS
1 16-OZ. CAN PINEAPPLE CHUNKS
1 10-OZ. JAR PRESERVED GINGER
2 LARGE ONIONS
4 WHOLE ORANGES
2 16-OZ. BOXES LIGHT BROWN SUGAR
2 15-OZ. BOXES YELLOW RAISINS
2 TEASPOONS GROUND CLOVES
2 TEASPOONS GROUND CINNAMON
1 TEASPOON SALT
1 TEASPOON CAYENNE PEPPER
3 CUPS CIDER VINEGAR

PEEL AND CORE PEARS. CUT INTO ½-INCH DICE. PLACE IN A KETTLE. COARSELY CHOP THE PINEAPPLE, GINGER, ONIONS AND ORANGES. PLACE THEM IN KETTLE WITH ALL OTHER INGREDIENTS.

BRING TO BOIL, SIMMER FOR 30 MINUTES. PLACE IN STERILIZED JARS AND SEAL.

T. ANSLEY

HE'S GOING TO MAKE **APPLE CRISP!**

6 TART APPLES
1 CUP SUGAR
1/4 TEASPOON GROUND CLOVES
1/2 TEASPOON CINNAMON
2 TEASPOONS LEMON JUICE
3/4 CUP SIFTED FLOUR
1/8 TEASPOON SALT
6 TABLESPOONS BUTTER
1/2 CUP WALNUTS, COARSELY CHOPPED
WHIPPING CREAM

PEEL, CORE AND SLICE APPLES. ADD 1/2 CUP SUGAR, THE SPICES AND LEMON JUICE. MIX AND PUT INTO A BUTTERED BAKING DISH. BLEND FLOUR, 1/2 CUP SUGAR, SALT, AND BUTTER TOGETHER.

ADD NUTS.

SPRINKLE EVENLY OVER APPLES AND BAKE IN A 350° OVEN FOR 45 MINUTES OR UNTIL BROWNED.
SERVE WITH WHIPPED CREAM.

2 SQUARES UNSWEET-
ENED CHOCOLATE
¼ POUND BUTTER
2 EGGS
1 CUP SUGAR
½ CUP FLOUR
1 CUP WALNUTS,
BROKEN
1 TEASPOON VANILLA

**M**ELT CHOCOLATE WITH BUTTER OVER LOW HEAT, COOL. BEAT EGGS AND SLOWLY ADD SUGAR. ADD CHOCOLATE AND OTHER INGREDIENTS AND MIX WELL. POUR INTO A GREASED 8-INCH BAKING PAN AND BAKE FOR 30 MINUTES IN A 350° OVEN. WHEN COOL, CUT INTO SQUARES.

# SWEDISH AFTERNOON DELIGHTS

2 cubes butter
1 cup brown sugar, packed
1 egg
3 cups flour
1 teaspoon baking powder
½ teaspoon baking soda
1 teaspoon cinnamon
1 teaspoon cardamom
1 cup almonds, finely chopped or ground, unblanched

CREAM BUTTER AND ADD OTHER INGREDIENTS. WORK INTO A DOUGH. FORM 1 INCH BALLS OF DOUGH AND PLACE ON UNGREASED COOKIE SHEET. PRESS EACH BALL WITH A FORK TO MAKE COOKIES.

BAKE IN A 350° OVEN FOR 10 MINUTES OR UNTIL NICELY BROWNED. COOL ON RACK AND PACK IN AIRTIGHT CONTAINER.

THESE AFTERNOON DELIGHTS ARE GREAT IN THE MORNING TOO!

## A SCANDINAVIAN FAVORITE
# CARDAMOM CAKE

| | | | |
|---|---|---|---|
| ½ | POUND BUTTER | | GRATED RIND OF 1 LEMON |
| 1 | CUP SUGAR | | GRATED RIND OF 1 ORANGE |
| 6 | EGGS, WELL BEATEN | 1 | TEASPOON VANILLA |
| 2 | CUPS ALL-PURPOSE FLOUR | 2 | TABLESPOONS SUGAR MIXED WITH, |
| 1 | TABLESPOON CARDA-MOM POWDER | 1 | TEASPOON CINNA-MON |
| 2 | TEASPOONS BAKING POWDER | | |
| 1 | CUP CURRANTS, STEAMED FOR SOFTNESS | | |

Using the low speed of a mixer, cream the butter and slowly add the sugar. Add eggs and beat well.

Sift flour, cardamom and baking powder together. Save a little of the flour to dust the currants.

ADD FLOUR MIXTURE TO THE BUTTER AND EGG MIXTURE. FOLD IN GRATED RINDS AND FLOURED CURRANTS. ADD VANILLA AND STIR WELL.

SPREAD BATTER IN A BREAD-LOAF PAN. SPRINKLE TOP WITH SUGAR-CINNAMON MIXTURE AND BAKE IN A 350° OVEN FOR ONE HOUR.

SERVE THIS CAKE THE NEXT DAY IF YOU CAN KEEP FROM EATING IT ON THE SPOT. YOUR KITCHEN WILL NEVER SMELL BETTER.

HE'S GOT NO WILL POWER.

F. ANSLEY

106

# Cornmeal Cookies

- ¼ POUND SOFT BUTTER
- ¾ CUP SUGAR
- 3 EGG YOLKS
- ¾ CUP CORN MEAL
- ¾ CUP FLOUR
- GRATED RIND OF 1 LEMON
- ¼ TEASPOON VANILLA

CREAM BUTTER AND SUGAR TOGETHER. ADD EGG YOLKS ONE AT A TIME, MIXING EACH ONE WELL. MIX CORN MEAL AND FLOUR TOGETHER AND ADD TO EGG YOLK MIXTURE. ADD LEMON RIND AND VANILLA.

SHAPE INTO A ROLL. WRAP IN WAX PAPER AND REFRIGERATE UNTIL HARD. CUT INTO ROUNDS A LITTLE LESS THAN ¼-INCH THICK. PLACE ON A BUTTERED COOKIE SHEET AND BAKE IN A 325° OVEN FOR 12 MINUTES OR UNTIL NICELY BROWNED.

REMOVE TO RACK AND COOL. STORE IN AIRTIGHT CONTAINER.

F. ANSLEY

# Crème Brulée

2 CUPS HEAVY CREAM
1 TEASPOON SUGAR
4 EGG YOLKS
1 TEASPOON VANILLA
3/4 CUP BROWN SUGAR

HEAT CREAM IN TOP OF DOUBLE BOILER, ADD SUGAR AND STIR UNTIL DISSOLVED.

BEAT EGG YOLKS AND STIR INTO HOT CREAM, ADD VANILLA AND POUR INTO BAKING DISH.

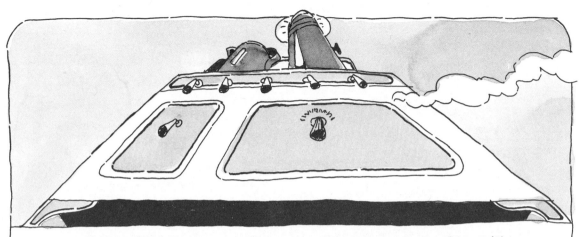

SET INTO PAN WITH 1 INCH OF HOT WATER AND BAKE IN A 300° OVEN FOR 50 OR 60 MINUTES, UNTIL AN INSERTED SILVER KNIFE COMES OUT CLEAN.

SIFT BROWN SUGAR OVER TOP AND SET UNDER BROILER UNTIL SUGAR CARAMELIZES. WATCH CAREFULLY TO PREVENT BURNING.

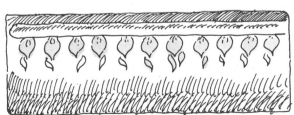

SERVE CHILLED.

NOT YOU, THE CRÈME BRULÉE!

109

NO. 1

## TO MAKE

# THE VERY BEST CUSTARD

- 6 TABLESPOONS BROWN SUGAR
- 4 EGGS
- 2 EGG YOLKS
- ½ CUP SUGAR
- 1 TEASPOON VANILLA
- 3 CUPS HALF AND HALF

HEAT BROWN SUGAR WITH A DROP OF WATER OVER VERY LOW HEAT UNTIL MELTED AND CARAMELIZED. POUR 1 TABLESPOON CARAMELIZED SUGAR INTO BOTTOM OF INDIVIDUAL CUSTARD CUPS.

BEAT EGGS AND EGG YOLKS WITH SUGAR AND VANILLA.

IN A LARGE BOWL WORK ALL INGREDIENTS EXCEPT WALNUTS INTO A DOUGH. FORM 1-INCH BALLS OF DOUGH AND PRESS A WALNUT HALF INTO EACH ONE.

¼ POUND BUTTER
¼ POUND MARGARINE
1 CUP SUGAR
1 CUP BROWN SUGAR
1 EGG, LIGHTLY BEATEN
1 TEASPOON VANILLA
½ TEASPOON SALT
1 TEASPOON BAKING SODA
1 TEASPOON BAKING POWDER
3 CUPS FLOUR
12-OZ. PACKAGE CHOCOLATE CHIPS
1 CUP SHREDDED COCONUT
WALNUTS

BAKE ON UNGREASED COOKIE SHEET FOR 12 MINUTES IN A 375° OVEN. LET COOL FOR 1 MINUTE BEFORE REMOVING TO RACK. WHEN COOL, STORE IN AN AIRTIGHT CONTAINER.

E. ANSLEY

113

# LEMON NUT COOKIES

## YOU'LL NEED:

- ½ POUND BUTTER
- 1 TEASPOON NUTMEG
- 2 CUPS SUGAR
- 2 EGGS
- 3 CUPS SIFTED ALL-PURPOSE FLOUR
- 2¼ CUPS WALNUT PIECES GRATED RIND OF TWO LEMONS

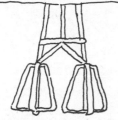

CREAM THE BUTTER AND ADD THE NUTMEG, SUGAR AND BEAT WELL. ADD THE EGGS ONE AT A TIME AND BEAT AFTER EACH.

GRADUALLY ADD THE FLOUR WHILE MIXING AND BEAT ONLY UNTIL MIXTURE IS SMOOTH. MIX IN THE NUTS AND LEMON RIND.

$Shape$ INTO A LONG ROLL WITH FLOURED HANDS AND WRAP IN WAX PAPER AND PUT INTO THE REFRIGERATOR. CHILL UNTIL VERY FIRM.

WHEN CHILLED, CUT DOUGH INTO ¼ INCH SLICES AND BAKE IN A 350° OVEN FOR 18 TO 20 MINUTES.

COOL COOKIES ON RACK!

MMMM COOK-IE!!

F. ANSLEY

IF YOU TAKE:

2 ENVELOPES UNFLAVORED GELATIN
2½ CUPS HOT WATER
2 CUPS SUGAR
½ CUP LEMON JUICE
4 EGGS, SEPARATED
2 TABLESPOONS FLOUR
3 CUPS MILK
1 TEASPOON VANILLA

WE'LL MAKE **LEMON SNOW!**

DISSOLVE GELATIN IN ½ CUP HOT WATER FOR 5 MINUTES.

MIX GELATIN WITH 2 CUPS HOT WATER, 1 CUP SUGAR AND LEMON JUICE. PLACE IN REFRIGERATOR UNTIL THICKENED.

BEAT EGG WHITES UNTIL STIFF AND FOLD INTO THICKENED GELATIN MIXTURE. PLACE IN WET CUSTARD CUPS, NON-METAL, AND PUT IN REFRIGERATOR UNTIL COLD AND SET.

MAKE A SAUCE IN TOP OF DOUBLE BOILER WITH 1 CUP SUGAR, EGG YOLKS, FLOUR, MILK.

COOK OVER HOT WATER UNTIL SAUCE COATS A SPOON. ADD VANILLA.

CHILL SAUCE AND SERVE OVER UNMOLDED GELATIN.

E. ANSLEY

..AND FOR DESSERT WE'LL HAVE A NICE **LIME PIE**

3 EGGS
1 15 OZ. CAN SWEETENED CONDENSED MILK
1/3 CUP LIME JUICE
1 BAKED PIE SHELL
1 CUP WHIPPING CREAM
2 TABLESPOONS SHERRY WINE
1 PINCH CINNAMON

SEPARATE EGGS AND BEAT YOLKS UNTIL LEMON COLORED. WHIP EGG WHITES UNTIL STIFF.

COMBINE MILK, LIME JUICE, AND EGG YOLKS.

## PRUNES IN PORT

THEY'VE ARRIVED

1 POUND PITTED PRUNES
2 CUPS PORT WINE
1 CUP RED WINE
½ CUP LIGHT BROWN SUGAR
6 WHOLE CLOVES
1 STICK CINNAMON
1 CUP HEAVY CREAM
1 TEASPOON VANILLA

COMBINE PRUNES, WINE, SUGAR, CLOVES AND CINNAMON. BRING TO BOIL. SIMMER 5 MINUTES.

SPOON INTO JARS AND LET STAND FOR 24 HOURS. REFRIGERATE. SERVE WITH WHIPPED CREAM FLAVORED WITH VANILLA.

# RUM CHOCOLATE MOUSSE ~

- ¼ CUP SUGAR
- 4 TABLESPOONS RUM
- 4 1-OZ. SQUARES SEMI-SWEET CHOCOLATE
- 2 TABLESPOONS STRONG COFFEE
- 2 EGG WHITES, BEATEN STIFF
- 1 CUP HEAVY CREAM, WHIPPED.

OVER VERY LOW HEAT, DISSOLVE THE SUGAR IN RUM. IN THE TOP OF A DOUBLE BOILER MELT THE CHOCOLATE WITH COFFEE.

BLEND THE TWO MIXTURES AND COOL. FOLD BEATEN EGG WHITES INTO THE CHOCOLATE MIXTURE. THEN FOLD IN WHIPPED CREAM.

SPOON INTO INDIVIDUAL DISHES. CHILL FOR 3 HOURS BEFORE SERVING.

## GET READY TO MAKE
# STRAWBERRY TART

1   3-OZ. PACKAGE CREAM CHEESE
3   TABLESPOONS CREAM
1   BAKED PIE SHELL
2   BOXES RIPE STRAWBERRIES
     ORANGE JUICE
1   CUP SUGAR
3   TABLESPOONS CORNSTARCH
     WHIPPING CREAM

BEAT CREAM CHEESE WITH CREAM. SPREAD OVER BOTTOM OF PIE SHELL. ARRANGE CLEANED STRAWBERRIES, TIP UP, IN PIE SHELL.

SIEVE REMAINING BERRIES AND ADD ORANGE JUICE TO MAKE 1 CUP.

MIX CORNSTARCH AND SUGAR WITH A LITTLE ORANGE JUICE AND ADD TO STRAINED BERRIES. COOK UNTIL CLEAR AND THICKENED. STIR OFTEN. POUR OVER STRAWBERRIES IN PIE SHELL AND CHILL.

SERVE WITH WHIPPED CREAM.

F. ANSLEY

# WINTER FRUIT

1 cup dried apricots
1 cup dried pitted prunes
2 bananas
½ cup raisins
½ cup walnuts, coarsely chopped
2 tablespoons butter
1 cup orange juice
4 tablespoons orange honey

SOAK DRIED FRUIT IN WARM WATER FOR 1 HOUR. DRAIN AND MAKE ROWS OF PRUNES, APRICOTS, SLICED BANANAS IN A SHALLOW BAKING DISH. SPRINKLE WITH RAISINS, CHOPPED NUTS AND DOT WITH BUTTER.

MIX ORANGE JUICE WITH HONEY AND POUR OVER FRUIT. BAKE IN A 350° OVEN FOR 40 MINUTES.

SERVE WITH CREAM, WHIPPED CREAM, SOUR CREAM OR ICE CREAM.

GREAT ANY SEASON OF THE YEAR!

# INDEX

# AUTHOR ROBERT STEFFY

Author Robert Steffy adds impetus to the growing theory that persons with an artistic nature show equally good taste in foods. He excels in both fields.

His romance with food began early, and he has been collecting recipes and cook books since before his graduation from Parsons' School of Design.

His idea for this book was to present to the novice, as well as the experienced cook, some good, simple recipes hoping to turn the reader onto the joys of cooking.

Mr. Steffy is a designer of furniture and other household-related items. For many years he has worked with manufacturers in Europe and is currently expanding into the awakening Oriental manufacturing fields, to give a truly international expression to his creative abilities.

# ARTIST FRANK ANSLEY

A special secret ingredient in any happy recipe is preparation enjoyment.

Artist Frank Ansley helps supply this in the Captain Cook cookbook.

His is not the tongue-in-cheek variety of humor, though. His tongue is obviously too busy licking his lips over the many innovative recipes... always ably aided by his own real cat, Ivan.

Born in Hibbing, Minnesota, reared in Detroit, and living in San Francisco's Bay Area since 1959 (except for 3 years in Los Angeles at the Art Center School, 1½ years in New York at an ad agency, and a year in Amsterdam, Holland doing free-lance illustrating), he developed a strong interest in good eating and food preparation.

He is currently living in Berkeley, California with his wife and daughter Sierra, and maintains a studio near the San Francisco waterfront. Here, too, he is inadvertently food-associated, he is located in the old Del Monte flour mill.